I sing sonnets & other forms:

about things everywhere

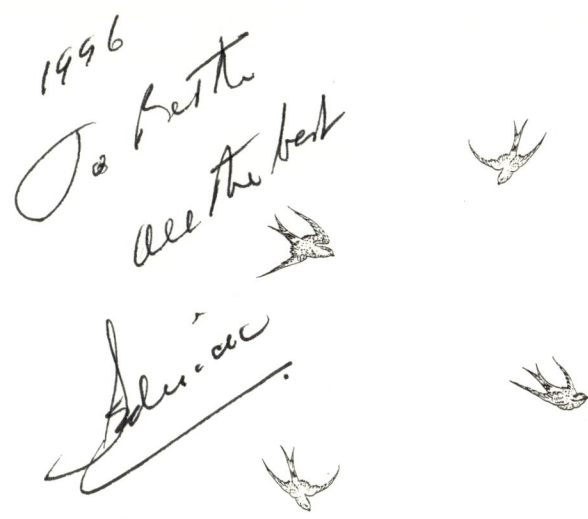

I sing sonnets & other forms:

about things everywhere

Sedrick Arlington Goldbeck
The Bird Press

First Printing

Copyright © 1996 in the U.S.A. by Sedrick A. Goldbeck
All rights reserved under International and Pan-American Copyright Conventions. Published in 1996 by The Bird Press.

Created and Designed by Sedrick A. Goldbeck and Anthony McPhatter.
Typeface Times New Roman.

Library of Congress Catalog Card Number: 96-96068

ISBN 0-9647881-0-1(PB)

Anthony McPhatter
Wilton Enterprises

Manufactured and Printed by:

Thompson-Shore
7300 West Joy Road
P.O Box 305
Dexter, MI 48130-0305

The Bird Press
658 East 227th Street
Bronx, NY 10466-3905

Acknowledgments . . .

my thanks and Love to my wife,
family, and friends
who read and patiently
listened.

special thanks to:

Bernard McMahon, teacher and mentor
Thomas Taafe, teacher
College of New Rochelle, New Resources
Milanez Walker (deceased), fellow poet and mentor
Jim Feast, The National Poetry Magazine of the Lower East Side
Robert Bailey, Poetry Live
Katherine (Images in Flight) and Kurt Lamkin, fellow poets
Mary Grace, Centerfold producer
Daniel Fernandez, Director, The New York Poetry Forum
A special thanks to E.K. for a last reading
Anthony McPhatter, Wilton Enterprises

Preface

This collection of fireballs by Sedrick A. Goldbeck beckons the readers' entrance with a golden hand. They are the mood pieces of a man who only breaks his mind to the world when his natural reticence is overpowered in bittersweet passion. As he suggests in " . . . Crazy after all these years," profound meditations do not lead him to a full articulation of his inner self. Only through writing can the fleeting flittings of his disrobed heart be recorded.

Yet, happily, once he breaks his mind through verse, he finds himself surrounded by those who are drawn to his song. Many of his writings express not only his emotions, but the way his expression of these emotions have been sustained by a company of like-minded spirits. Many of the poems in this book are testimonies, like raised glasses, to those who, with him uphold the light of poetry in our times.

This is only one theme in the jewel box of this volume. But there is one underlying message which would seem to be: <u>Poetry deepens the glance</u>. Whatever the subject, whether mysticism, friends or love, Goldbeck sets forward thoughtful observations and intimations.

To take one example, look at the special attention paid to the wind. In no less than three pieces, the poet looks at the breeze, which, he contends, is as moody as his own soul. In "The Winds," breezes are, by turns, dreary, daffy, cheering or dripping with venomous emotions as they often are with rain.

Like the English Romantics, whose writings have nurtured Goldbeck, he sees a full-fledged intermingling of nature and human life, which appears most clearly in breezes; since they are closest to humans in being discernibly and effervescently modifiable according to changing conditions. Unlike the Romantics, however, Goldbeck sees the dark side of nature as much as he celebrates its positive aspects. Winds have forbidding, rowdy aspects, viewable in storms that destroy and "uproot."

This should be enough to indicate the fullness of the poet's glance, which in condensed imagery, pearl-encrusted language and sinuous thought always gives one more than what one expects. A poet whose power can never be anticipated and never possessed.

Jim Feast

CONTENTS

I

Past Cure, Past Care

Fork & Knife   5
Londontown: Hadrian's Wall   6
Mary Grace   7
These Buildings   8

II

And Yet We Err

Destiny   11
In Death there is life   12
Drug called Ecstacy   13
So hold me Moros   14
What seek you?   15

III

Love You, Love You, love you

Crazy   19
Crystal or Ash   20
Dare to say   22
For two friends   23
Jewel in the lotus   24
Love in endless rhymes   25
Love's counterpoint   26
Tides in the affairs of men   27
Wedding toast   28
Your love to me   29
Where every promise lies   30

IV

Like Chaos, Like the Road Ahead

Fickle muse   33
Need of sonnets flow   34
Those chickens home to roost   35

V

The Seasons

Four season's sonnets   39
Perfumed breath of spring   40
Heat of summer's rays   41
Come now you fall   42
Oh come sweet winter's sleep   43

VI

Survival: the battle to live

After all   47
And so you winds   48
Forbidden Omens   49
Hollow Passions   50
Jazz   51
Let the play begin   52
The winds   53
Things I remember best   54
Time Flew   55

Finis   57

Notes on the Author   59

I sing sonnets & other forms:

about things everywhere

I

PAST CURE, PAST CARE

Past cure I am, now reason is past care,
and frantic mad with evermore unrest,
My thoughts and my discourse as madness are . . .

Sonnet 147
Wm. Shakespeare

FORK & KNIFE

You sometimes hesitate when eating out
to order the very thing you like the best;
The menu scrolls entrees, perhaps broiled trout,
Loin lambchops, veal or sweetbreads, but your test
(and some chef's demise), is to try instead
his burgers's; Are they juicy, sweet & rare
or dry & hard or just plain dead deaddead,
or fries french crisp & soft beyond compare?
However, for that, you do not pant or sigh,
you want to taste some crunchy succulence,
perhaps a chicken wing, a breast or thigh;
a platter high, intense with such abundance.

>So dig in quickly, taste the joys of life-
>Use your fingers, forget the fork & knife.

LONDONTOWN: Hadrian's Wall

Fifteen were we, with eyes and ears awake
　we plan to gorge and feast and fill our dreams
　with Londontown; we want to stop and stare
at streets, and walk long walks of history-
to share its pulse now vibrant young, but once
so old its stones so cold; and all will come
alive for us; see Henry, James and Charles
all Kings come forth to wile and entertain.

But then, compare the bit of Hadrian's wall
unearthed, exposed so preciously set and framed
amidst the glass and steel and stone; see smoke
exhausts from buses, cars like death to drift
and darken suns that shined for years long past-
Still shine.　Still hear the voices old and new.

To Mary Grace, Producer of the Centerfold Coffeehouse, after witnessing a short presentation of her songs, August 4, 1987

MARY GRACE.

There is an Angel voice in Centerfold,
A lyric voice of delicate sweetness-
Whose music heard brings blessing sevenfold
And charms all those who stay to witness.
Her magic lies in impish songs of humor
Or sounds the misery and pain of Blues;
She plucks the strings of hearts and so the rumor
That she is conjurer, magician, Muse.

But no, I know she is not any of these-
And still, her voice will capture all who hear.
Please wait, just rest a moment at your ease-
While time moves quick and tunes caress your ear.

> So sit you down at Centerfold in place
> And hear the angel voice of Mary Grace.

THESE BUILDINGS

All march along like soldiers on the make-
(In shadows see lights pick and choose to glow)
And clouds surround and wait as at a wake;
Then stop, remain in place for twilight's flow-
Declare, 'we'll stay right here for night to grow-
For day to take its leave and night retrieve.'
While earth keeps turning day to night-a slow
Dance dark in melting softness starts to weave.

Thus round these buildings, lo do I perceive
This rendezvous-a shift from day to night;
Glass eyes that spot like fireflies in the eve-
See cycles day to night a ritual rite.

So on this screen with background sky I see
Again within some light this play to be.

II

AND YET WE ERR

we melt, and plan how to act
in order to avoid the certain
danger so frightfully menacing us.
And yet we err, it is not in our paths:
the messages were false alarms . . . .

Finalities
Cavafy

DESTINY

In this spare darkness do I walk with wonder-
To seek the truths perchance I should not hear;
And come to know my destiny a traveler-
To see the light and hear the voice I fear.
There Aion, lion deity, huge wings
Outspread - its serpent's eyes affixed on me,
And roaring voice rings loud with echoings
Against the walls-and Aion says, "I see
You've traveled far to know if heav'n or hell
Will make you theirs. Good patience bids you wait
Until your time is come, and when the bell
resounds aloud you'll learn your future state;

        Perhaps return to ashes, dust, and soul
        To rest according to the ancient scroll."

IN DEATH THERE IS LIFE

And Death in time comes riding up from Hell
To tempt or claim those waiting there for him.
All stand in trembling at the Devil's whim
Perchance to hear the tolling of the bell.
But fate no certainty as time will tell
May send mixed blessings with the Cherubim,
Bring Death or joyful songs of Seraphim.
In Death there's Life and Life in Death will Dwell-
Transactions all - a change to something new;
Our lives fulfill according to some plan.
Weep not at Death - Rejoice with great elan
To end one life, another life renew;

       In gardens sow - where every seed will be
       A fresh beginning of new things for thee.

DRUG CALLED ECSTASY

Cute and pert and blond, short skirt and boots
that's what she wears, with pen in hand she writes
of loveless pairings pushed high to fall
with Ecstasy, a new one voted best;
it bested all the others for awhile-
to lift the shades and stretch beyond the sun-
and Love is now not what it seems to be
no longer chaste or sweet but outward bound.

She smiles and asks, "have you tried Ecstasy?"
With half-closed eyes, she whispers, "try it Love."
And those who count upon such Love induced,
now tread the Stygian shores with empty arms,
    or those whose destiny courts death-
      an earthly class of lovers who in light
      Create in ignorance their own ecstasy.

SO HOLD ME MOROS

My heart is stilled, my body icy chilled
Hears winter's winds, a draft, a cold caress.
So dry leaves yellow, russet, brown are willed
On currents swift of swirling air to dress
The covered paths; while trees, their branches bare
Create designs against the winter's sky.
And in this loneliness my soul waits there
To faintly hear a call - the Lorelei
Whose calling cries to tempt me to her bier;
There she will hold my heart, while singing sweet
Those things that I have waited, longed to hear.
But too late, for those words and voices meet
And I know Death is nigh - a happy keep.

So hold me Moros - Son of Night to sleep.

WHAT SEEK YOU?

*hat seek you*, look for in this world-Lost Dreams?
Where are those known and unknown things you
seek?
You seem despaired your eyes beclouded bleak;
You read too much those histories in reams
That bind your eye, your mind convulsed it seems-
> Your thoughts now dry, your dreams have lost
> mystique,
> > Those cloud-built, youthful swellings now seem weak
You tend your dreams now by some quiet streams.

Thus lay he there at rest with eyes now dim,
> His beard is grey, his limbs are tired and worn.
What dreams he now-some melody, some hymn?
> A song he hears with words that call to mourn;
This sadness that he feels - Do they mourn him?
> Is this a dream perhaps before the morn?

III

LOVE YOU, Love You, love you

   Come on drink cognac.
    Rather have wine?
   Come Here, I love you.
    Come and be mine.

      Port Town
      Langston Hughes

CRAZY

As twilight steals to night and darkened sleep-
My eyelids closed - at rest and still I see
Light figures dance before my eyes carefree.
But I am not so free, within I keep
My feelings deep, so I write - never reap
The prizes others win who seem more free,
Or lightly play the game of Love - but flee
Attachments long or firm and never weep . .

Then suddenly from sky and clouds there's you;
A match in reticence that so endears-
I cannot help but drop my guard, undo
My JuJu safety net - see wide frontiers-
And games I loathe - we play a Love's hoodoo,
And I'm "still crazy after all these years."

"CRYSTAL OR ASH.
FIRE OR WIND AS LONG AS IT'S LOVE."
Lena Wertmuller

1.

ithout embellishment some Love can be like Ash
or Crystal Fire or Wind as natural as Love
can be a diamond in its beauty cut to shine
secure in its own design flashing moments high
and blindly turn each flattened side to catch the light
but shy this Love with bent refractions, stumbling words
two minds have met and dared these feelings to fulfill
they step together measured step by step with dreams . . .

But dreams are not enough and mirrors give an empty cup
for know this Love a taboo holds that wishful thoughts
will not transport along the twisted path called Love
however Love when felt so diademed would seem
to be a blind fierce Mistral wind and so join those
who need to feel beyond the closeness of a kiss.

2.

This kiss that holds and transports some along the path
called Love can justly fill your soul and under tongue
can weaken knees spell blindness with an L or O
a V an E but Oh you thrill for this and want
it more a craving want beyond safe limits reach
and dare compare the turnings of two hearts more like
fire of sticks that spark and sing of Spring while April's
crystals shower endless wet on this event . . .

But Love as Crystals shine may burn like comet stars
then die revive rebuild itself to star again
in years to come or soon right now as embers glow
so walk walk quickly into grasping flames of Dante's
Hell as stages grow without fair Beatrice to
guide through Fire or Wind as long as it is Love.

DARE TO SAY

I dare to say I Love without knowing
If you are privy to the things I feel;
And know all questions without my asking,
Sift through my mind, its secrets to reveal.
This page, a diary of thoughts, my Love,
Emotions, words and lines not timorous
Will make the fool feel braver yet; whereof
In dreamlike fantasy, I dream of us
With earthly fortunes gleaming in the light
Amid the luxury that day dreams will allow-
As we search for treasures to delight
And with much pleasure find the golden bough,

>My tree to your so gentle wind will bend,
>With words of Love and friendship . . .

>>friend to friend.

23

... to Cat and Kurt for May 20th, 1989.

FOR TWO FRIENDS

For two friends, Lovers of words as I do love
them too - I'll try to weave this sonnet with
familiar words and phrases of these two,
and wish for them a house to house their Love
her brownstone building 5 x 4 filled full
5 stories tall - 4 windows wide of Love
of her, her warmth, her body food, her soul
replete with dreams and arms to hold him close
while he imagines images of Love
where he is free to see horizons that
become his sea at dusk or love at dawn
with God supreme to help fulfill the plan.

    They have the stuff to make it all come true
    to conjure it in faith - their Love renew.

JEWEL IN THE LOTUS

And love, a tender fruit of ripeness taste
Will fill your mind with clouds, and give much heat.
You spend the day in idle dreams and waste
Sweet time, have sleepless nights and thoughts replete
With sparkling Jewels; so the prophecy-
To smell the Lotus - feel the flowing tides
Fulfill you as you moan with ecstasy-
While Pegasus plunges deeply-wildly rides.

Then listen - hear the hum, the Mantra sound:
Hear chanters chant, "Om mani padme hum."
And so with mind entranced you lie spellbound:
And hear repeated, "Om mani padme hum,"

>The rosary of Love - now surrender
>To dream - the dreamings of the slumberer.

LOVE IN ENDLESS RHYMES

You need not write of Love in endless rhymes
Of blood that whips around a rolling boil-
And hearts that beat or miss a beat sometimes,
    Of sleepers blessed and touched with 'Voodoo Oil.'
Love's 'Voodoo Oil' from which all souls recoil-
    Whose fingers touch your flesh - cause you to burn.
    Your Eden's sleep filled with a Serpent's coil-
    Full terrors see for which the gargoyles yearn.
Those tears you shed or smiles - try to unlearn;
    They are not worth the pain or joy you feel-
    Emotions laid on someone's strange epergne
    To pick or choose in momentary zeal.

So wave good-bye to Love, be not spellbound,
    For you exist for more than Love unsound.

LOVE'S COUNTERPOINT

The heat of Summer's rays they fancy you-
Helps flowers, trees to grow and blossom there.
Wet nectar on your body tastes like dew-
    and sweetness of your perfume fills the air.
See birds and bees flit here and everywhere
    To carry Love's true potions and the news.
    Hear one and all, let none be unaware
    That sultry breezes come to light Love's fuse.
A kiss to Love whose special words transfuse
    A fetish charm - cause rivers wild to run
    With fires of Love so strong-it will infuse
    The powerful force primeval that you've won.

Remember Spring just past the starting point
    Of Love to end - begin Love's counterpoint.

'... TIDES IN THE AFFAIRS OF MEN ...'

So *Love at* full 'tide in the affairs of men'
and women runs its course in all—the same;
each step to raise the moments heat will build
no matter far or near, the fragrance will
cross land and air—give to their love a smell
intense in flavor at its utmost peak;
if not fulfilled will cool—diffuse its heat.
How can you know when beat of heart or pulse
means love in depth—or flights of fancy
in passions eye a weaker gem to hold?
Know well, this tide will not allow you license
to run away get free—will clasp you fast,
and mire your feet to wait for love's true
joinings One to One and Breath to Breath.

WEDDING TOAST

And now to smiling Bride and Groom we toast,
With wishes that your smiles will ever be
As joyful as this day remembered - most
Of all your future days that we foresee.
In years ahead we see your lives unfold:
To find you captured in your Love as one-
A perfect plan, design, a Marriage mold,
That holds you closer when Life's battles won.
We pray that blessings touch you from above
With magic, fresh as Springtime's morning dew,
That casts its spell to keep you both in Love.

>So try to keep it constant, always new-
>An endless Love to hold and treasure,
>And live your lives fulfilled in pleasure.

YOUR LOVE TO ME

Your *Love to* me, a strong and heady drink,
Does not assuage or quench my burning thirst.
The kisses stolen form your lips, I think
Provoke within - an emptiness, accursed.
I truly dream of you (will dreams suffice?)
Of keys to priceless treasures out of sight.
Your Love I sorely need, my soul like ice
Needs only lie within your warmth and might-
To burn with fires of Love that you entice.
My dreams, your dreams I know are both the same,
To see this crazy madness more concise.

Need Love ignite in such a raging flame
To exorcize our demons - and so condemn
      Us, leave us naked at our Requiem?

WHERE EVERY PROMISE LIES

I awake now every morning, and it's you,
I sleep you in my mind, your body mine.
Recall flirtatious scenes when you did woo
With heat from fingers traced against her spine,
A fair young Miss, and seem to overcome.
She did accept, while still she kept her space.
And I observed this play, which in large sum
Allowed that you were expert, with much grace.

My body felt your touch, and trembled there,
I saw that questioning look-you always look
Then smelt your scent as sweet as flowers wear.
You seem so wise - I wonder and I book,

> Your line, your baited hook will catch the prize,
> Fulfill this game where every promise lies.

IV

LIKE CHAOS, LIKE THE ROAD AHEAD

Limb tongue, and sinew into a knot
Like chaos, like the road
ahead.

The Swamp
Derek Walcott

FICKLE MUSE

So *the gentle* Muse, words trailing in her wake,
Thinks you undeserving of her pleasures—
Hoarding words - then she may give you one to take—
Wine or dine you with these sumptuous treasures.
See words shine and sparkle like a brilliant,
hear words breathe - sing praise to high heaven.
Feel words hard, unyielding and resilient
Then light words that to dark dreams add leaven.
Sense the smell of words that calm all anger—
Draw their nectar - taste a honey sweet;
Soothing, they give feelings of such languor
Bringing enemies round tables all to meet.

    This prize is yours, but if you claim too late,
    The fickle Muse will leave you to your Fate.

NEED OF SONNETS FLOW

My free wheeling thoughts compress, and now
(In tightly woven form they want to read)
Words that flow as free verse - feels the need
of sonnets flow line stopped to listen, bow;
Words with rhyming endings, lines in metered beat.
And drumming beats in memory will lay
Held in thoughtful banks, cause all who may—
to sing in chorus, shouting words that greet,
Words that flay, composed in anger or then play
for smiles or sweetly drip with love or hate.
Words of truth may march and rush oncoming fate—
but then, like rivers dammed to stop halfway;

Just so you will remember and recount
those things recalled, occasions to surmount.

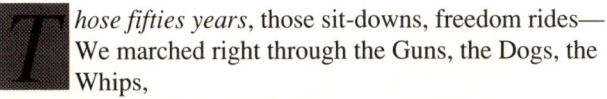

THOSE CHICKENS HOME TO ROOST

Those fifties years, those sit-downs, freedom rides—
We marched right through the Guns, the Dogs, the Whips,
The church that God watched over, now abides
With tears to weep for bloodied heads and lips.
Those children buried under hate and love,
When bombs were thrown to gain a change of heart,
to keep all Whites so pure a blessed dove—
But then black hearts and thoughts set them apart.
They claim to be humane to all so wise,
And soon forget our Luther, Malcolm now
They're dead - but they will in impatience rise
In peace or rage to taste rewards somehow—

      To pray, to wait unless our spirits boost,
      Then we will send those chickens home to roost.

# V

THE SEASONS

As space creates all things out of its own substance only to devour them again at last, so time which itself cannot move or change allots to everything its span of life. Our hours and days are within us and it is the revolution of the globe, and not time which makes the seasons.

The Forest Giant
Adrien Le Corbeau

FOUR SEASONS' SONNETS

pring precedes summer, fall and winter too
they follow one another, yes, that's true
so read these sonnets, feel the season's change
and then recapture moments, not so strange . . .
I will present you to some sprites divine
to fill your eye and mind with their design
but do not fear these dreams, it's all in fun
and you will smile, sweet smiles when all is done

PERFUMED BREATH OF SPRING

When eye meets eye and looks and lingers there,
And pulse of blood in heart and throat feel near;
We see a wall of love to breach so high,
To lose ourselves complete, and wonder why.
We feel sweet nectar, wet upon our lips,
And so on wings of fancy dream this bliss.
The light and tender touch with which Love grips;
That new and breathless feel of Spring's first kiss.
That soaring feeling wrapped in May's moonlight—
Takes tongue and mind and sense when dreams hold sway—
Come mid-Summer's madness, sweet with such delight.
So do not doubt good reasons Love this May.

> For still my Love you hold, I hold this thing
> That seems so light, a perfumed breath of Spring.

HEAT OF SUMMER'S RAYS

The heat of Summer's rays, they fancy you;
helps flowers, trees to grow and blossom there.
The moisture from your body tastes like dew,
And sweetness of your perfume scents the air,
So birds and bees flit here and everywhere
To carry Love's true potions and the news.

To one and all, let none be unaware,
That sultry breezes come to tempt the Muse
Full bloom to Love - creative juices flow
In you, and you hold fast while rivers run
Full of Love's fires that set you all aglow.
So feel the force primeval that you've won.

        Remember Spring just past, the starting point,
        Renewal of our birth, Love's counterpoint.

COME NOW YOU FALL

ome now you fall, hot Summer's rays to tame;
With fingers cool, stay Love a warm hot breath
Till twilight comes, and cherubs with faint aim
Shoot arrows, miss your heart and spare you Death.
Those arms await to hold you close, too close
to seal your eyes with lips-and so now blind
Your ears will hear sweet music, words verbose,
That crowd your mind, leave senses all behind.

So come Oh Mistress Love, with scent so sweet—
Please change your ghastly mask of Death I see.
For time is swift and moves so quick to meet
my Specter waiting, all that's left of me.

    See there a glow, a radiance far above
    While in death's arms, my Specter waits for Love.

OH COME SWEET WINTER'S SLEEP

Oh come sweet Winter's sleep, to me attend,
Your fingers put me down to rest, to sleep.
The flowers felt your touch at Summer's end
And bend themselves, their colors fade and weep.
The birds and bees all sleep or fly away
to find the Sun with rays of warmth again.
They leave this wonderland, where fairies play
A beauteous Winter view all words avow.
So ride the icy winds while hailstones dance—
for Sun and cold and wet are needed now,
To feed roots/seedlings, give new lives a chance.

    So come dear Spring, renew Love's lives to be
    With warming breezes, give new life to me.

VI

SURVIVAL: the battle to live

we fight to live beyond the battle
of the present and our past . . .
Some chill and succumb
others feel the warmth of life—
try to grasp its pulsing entrails
and live to fulfill
the symbols there . . .

Author

AFTER ALL

After all, this world is a masked ball
a Verdian " . . .Ballo in Maschera:"
With faces that are not theirs at all;

And who were they before the fall
now to speak words ex cathedra—
After all this world, is a masked ball;

Some mix together, sleepwalk from dawn to nightfall
play music & dance then turn macabre—
With faces that are not theirs at all;

Why there are Black, White, Short & Tall
& Brown, & Yellow, & Red races et cetera
After all this world, is a masked ball;

Some smile dark smiles & with sweet talk enthrall
& act out this scenario of life so ephemera—
With faces that are not theirs at all;

And frankly, I wonder if before the fall
the Garden described was real in true tempera—
After all, the world is a masked ball
With faces that are not theirs at all.

AND SO YOU WINDS

And so you winds that whip
    the waves on ship and shore
Or bring deathly silence
        the peace before the storm;

Cease these words repeating
    the reaching - whispering voice
That carries all - forgotten dreams
    or haunting memories.

And keep your Sirocco wind
    from me - the dust - the dirt
The sand that veils the eye
    then kills the breath.

Send fresh, the cleansing breeze
    quickly tingling - touching bold
To reach and hold - intwine
    insist itself around me.

FORBIDDEN OMENS

You twist and turn and cannot seem to rest
While things run through your mind from long ago.
The shirt is tight, its threads now turned suggest

    A grater 'gainst your body like steel wool - so
Gives you dreams unpleasant and unblessed.

    Those things so far away and let go
Are now awake in vivid wrappings there
Appear forbidden omens in life's glare.

HOLLOW PASSIONS

Your Love is not so passionate, so bold—

It once roared fires like a lioness

To make the coldest heart too hot to hold.

But memory serves you much soberness

'Gainst hollow passions without tenderness.

JAZZ

Jazz plays and sounds in different forms
to steal its way into your soul.

Listen! Hear the music played in storms—

Jazz plays and sounds in different forms,

      horns that echo, prancing beats in swarms.

There's jazz for all—Be-Bop, Blues and Creole

Jazz; plays and sounds in different forms.

So listen here! Just Hear it, try it—

      Lose Control.

LET THE PLAY BEGIN

et the play begin - the air caress your body tune

Sense the calm - the tenseness of the moment;

Then ride the tide - feel tightening pressures, and soon

Your body keened for sudden pleasures - dreams foment;

Those things from which you thought yourself immune

Are verdant, liquid, cataclysmic - a wild figment;

So let the play begin and let your body croon—

When dreams hold sway - you feel the organ grinder's tune.

THE WINDS

The winds sometimes are strange
They whistle, scream in pain
Then slowly, softly sing
Or swirl around and play.

They whistle, scream in pain
Mourn for the gore they leave
Or swirl around and play
Destruct, uproot that's all.

They soon complete their tasks
Then slowly, softly sing
Or funnel through the skies
Swiftly—on the wing.

Their breaths so fiercely felt
Hot-Cold they blow in day
Or night directions fly
All Ancient routes in arcs.

Hot-Cold they blow in day
Some narrow paths do take
All ancient routes in arcs
That sweep across the skies.

They sometimes croon and romp
And night directions fly
Their deeds they soon forget
These Winds sometimes are strange.

THINGS I REMEMBER BEST

Things I remember best when I was young—
    A park with grass so green or snow so white.
A beacon seen at night, a street light.
    Men with fur hats and slim dogs high strung—

White men with white dogs speaking a foreign tongue;
    That was Spring and Summer, not Winter's sight.
Things I remember best when I was young—
    A park with grass so green or snow so white.

Yes! Winter's cap so dense, so loosely flung
    From unknown heights, and day seen half-light;
And sounds at night are muffled—seem so finite.
    Things I remember best when I was young—
    A park with grass so green or snow so white.

TIME FLEW

Time flew - slipped away and left
cherished hills and rocks they loved bereft;

No more laughter - children's voices hear
or mother's, father's screams or pains to bear;

No more gaseous fumes, bullets, stones to maim
all gone - no man or woman, child in pain.

The flowers now will sleep and grow in peace
and insects, birds sweet voices find release;

> Altars bloodied - where all died to reconcile—
> Death now cools - words and feelings volatile.

Time flew - like winds of memories and offings swift
past bloody confrontations - give all short shrift.

And histories, futures, people symbiotic to the end—
all die for Heart and Will to gain a peaceful end.

FINIS

Canto xxv

... for he who rests on down
or under covers cannot come to fame;
and he who spends his life without renown
leaves such a vestige of himself on earth
as smoke bequeaths to air or foam to water.

Inferno
Dante Alighieri

Notes about the author . . .

A Certified Social Worker, born December 10, 1925, in New York, N.Y., he retired as a Domestic Foreign Service officer with the U.S. Information Agency in 1980. Worked in retail sales until January 1986, then attended the College of New Rochelle, graduating with a B.A. in the Humanities May 1989; and graduated from the Smith College School for Social Work in August 1991 with a Masters degree in Social Work, Practicing as a clinical social worker at a mental health clinic, he also has a private practice and completed some training as a family therapist. His poems have appeared in: American Poetry Association, Amelia, Black masks, "42", a Musty Bone, N.Y., the National Poetry Magazine of the Lower East Side, and in the Pyramid Periodical, N.Y. A Member of the N.Y. Poetry Forum, he has been a featured poet at their poetry meetings. He has appeared on Poetry Live, a cable program in New York. He studied with William Packard at New York University. Married, he has two adult children.

S. A. G.

Bronx,
New York